About the Author

M. L. Gelman is a medical doctor who was born and grew up in Zimbabwe where he practised as a Specialist Physician. Latterly he moved to Britain with his wife and worked in the NHS until retirement. He now lives in rural Cornwall. He has written a number of medical articles including a monograph titled *Traditional Medicine in Zimbabwe* and a book *Reflections of a Sceptic.*

Reflections
...the Human Dilemma

M.L Gelman

I dedicate this booklet to my wife Ann
and our three children, Sarah, Tammy and Mark.

Matador
9 Priory Business Park,
Wistow Road, Kibworth Beauchamp,
Leicestershire, LE8 0RX
Tel: 0116 279 2299
Email: books@troubador.co.uk
Web: www.troubador.co.uk/matador
Twitter: @matadorbooks

ISBN 978 1838591 298

British Library Cataloguing in Publication Data.
A catalogue record for this book is available from the British Library.

Printed and bound by CPI Group (UK) Ltd, Croydon, CR0 4YY
Typeset in 10.5pt Ten Oldstyle by Troubador Publishing Ltd, Leicester, UK

Matador is an imprint of Troubador Publishing Ltd

Aphorisms

Subjective interpretations of Time...

And time there on Planet Auschwitz, was not like time here. Each moment there revolved around the cogwheels of a different time-sphere. Hell-years last longer than light years.

Yechiel De Nur

The only reason for time is so that everything doesn't happen at once.

Albert Einstein

Life is like driving a car with the front windscreen opaque. All you have to go by are your rear-view mirrors. This is how we are all destined to navigate our lives.

Original unknown

More Einstein...

A human being is part of a whole called by us the Universe.

Education is not the learning of facts, it is rather the training of minds to think.

All that is valuable in human society depends on the opportunity for development accorded the individual.

It has become appallingly obvious that our technology has succeeded our humanity.

Winston Churchill...

It has been said that democracy is the worst form of government except for all the others that have been tried.

Success is not final, failure is not usually fatal; it is the courage to continue that counts.

South African Truth Commission...

Truth must precede Justice before Punishment, proceeding variably to Mercy and exceptionally to Forgiveness on the part of the aggrieved.

Know thyself ...

from the Temple of Apollo at Delphi.

Contents

Prologue

The purpose of this work is ambitious aiming to explore some of the limits of human awareness and provide perspective on our existence, the vastness of the universe, the unfathomable mysteries of space and time, the flux of elements from which all matter, animate and inanimate is composed, entering and leaving our bodies, altering the composition of our cells which continuously repair and regenerate adhering to a specific lattice which is in each of us determined at conception by our inherited DNA. Although we may periodically zoom out to the limits of our perception we have to withdraw to the more comfortable dimensions of our planet, forever our yardstick of space and time. It is intended to highlight the kinship which binds all mankind and the necessity to know the origins of the attitudes and emotions which periodically divide us, prompt us to destroy each other and our works and at other times lay down our lives and labour tirelessly for one another. We share many impulses with our animal ancestors such as a preoccupation with territory, clan loyalty, social hierarchy and sexuality which are built into our psyche and if recognised can be modified and channelled positively to our communal benefit. I hope to create an understanding of the urgent need for us all to recognise that we are part of the human family and to use our considerable intellect to create peace and prosperity for humankind. Utopia is perhaps still within our reach but time is short and through greed and ignorance we are squandering our fast-fading opportunity to repair the world. I will attempt to distinguish what is true and what is false, what is knowable and what we have yet to learn. It is sometimes better to continue to question than to assume an answer. I acknowledge that the issues I attempt to address form a tiny fraction of the growing complexity of human life and culture.

Our Galaxy

Our sun is one star of over 200 million within our galaxy we call the Milky Way (galaxy is a word derived from Greek *galaxios* meaning milk). As we are unable to take a 'selfie' of our home galaxy we make do with the image of our 'cosmic twin' without a name as yet but referred to as NGC 6744, similar in form although larger than our Milky Way, an estimated 30 million light years away, 100,000 light years in diameter and one of over 100 billion galaxies, consisting of stars, star remnants, dust, gas and 'dark matter' (not emitting nor reflecting light), comprising the Universe. Whether there are other, perhaps infinite numbers of Universes is still being debated.

The Blue Planet

Ours is a blue planet patched with green, yellow and white... blue because molecules of oxygen and nitrogen in the atmosphere and water in the oceans absorb red light from sunlight and reflect the blue. Green represents vegetation, yellow the deserts and white the clouds and polar ice-caps. As a planet reflecting blue light signals the likely presence of life-supporting oxygen and water only a blue planet can support life as we know it. Are there other blue planets in the vastness of the universe? Astronomers recently think they caught sight of one circling a distant star many light years away. The blue light-reflecting, life-supporting elements constitute the merest veneer on the surface of our Earth. It is so thin that an analogy is called for in order to comprehend how superficial is the veneer over the mantle of rock and core of iron. The diameter of the earth is approximately 12,800km, the air is breathable by migrating birds up to 8km above sea level. The soil and the life it bears is no more than 500 meters deep and the average ocean depth is 3.7km. The life sustaining veneer is thus no more than 13km deep and the ratio of veneer to the Earth's mantle and core approximately 13: 12,800. If the Earth is represented by an 8cm apple the veneer referred to would be thinner than the cuticle, the outer layer of the apple skin, 80hundredths of a millimetre (80micrometres or microns), the diameter of a fine human hair. Could this slender veneer represent the sum total of life in the universe? Whether one concurs or not with the possibility, we humans are part of the web of life and have become the custodians. Too few of us are aware of this responsibility to which is tied the fate of our children and of humankind.

Life in the Universe

Are we, inhabitants of Planet Earth alone in the Universe or an exceedingly rare phenomenon? Or is life more ubiquitous than anyone imagines, 'seed' borne by asteroids or meteorites, celestial messengers, pollen-bearers of the Universe. The seeds dispersed at random, sucked into fiery solar furnaces or striking bare planetary landscapes too hot or cold or dry, lacking atmosphere or seethed by cosmic radiation or more fortuitously landing on a 'Blue Planet' such as ours or life-friendly moon? Earth-bound, we might perceive such hypothetical good fortune to be exceedingly rare but amongst billions of stars/suns there would likely be millions possessed of planets with potential to support life. Would life then appear spontaneously or is a visit from a 'messenger' carrying 'seed' necessary? Is Life/Evolution pre-programmed in some celestial 'blueprint'? The answers to such mysteries are likely to remain forever beyond our reach and comprehension. We can only ponder the imponderable, dream and use our considerable earthly intelligence to work towards a better world.

Time

Time is without mass, cannot be weighed and measured objectively only in relation to some event or traversal over a given distance. Most commonly we understand time in relation to the rotation of the earth on its axis, it's orbit around the sun or the orbit of the moon around the earth. Time is otherwise subjective and it may be questioned whether it exists at all without reference to a progression of events. In a theoretical limitless empty void time has no relevance. Within the observable universe, time and distance are so immense as to have scant relevance. Only within our solar system and specifically on Planet Earth is time meaningful. For us, earthbound, time is real.

Cosmos versus Chaos...is there a 'blueprint'?

Acceptance that Cosmos is a state of order appears persuasive that there is a 'plan' which implies a guiding universal consciousness of some kind? The alternative hypothesis that an ordered universe exists through chance alone is virtually a contradiction equivalent to throwing up a bagful of letters of the alphabet an infinite number of times in the belief that these ultimately will fall into a readable form as the Works of Shakespeare, the Koran or whatever!

Time Line of Life

A grasp of time may be assisted by relating time since life began on Earth to the familiar 1 year. The scale starts at 3.5 billion years, 1 billion years since the presumed time of the formation of the Earth equating to January 1st, starting with simple anaerobic life forms. The pace was desultory with slow progress between June and September when photosynthesis speeded up the process with oxygenation of the atmosphere by early October. The Cambrian Period in early November heralded an 'explosion of life' including the entry of arthropods. Air-breathers appeared in mid-November and emerged on land as amphibians and reptiles in the heavily forested Carboniferous Period at the end of November. The Jurassic in early December saw the emergence of huge dinosaurs and small mammals, the former destroyed by and the latter survived the 'Great Extinction' attributed to asteroids striking the Earth. Early primates appeared around Xmas Day. The pace was accelerating, 27th December saw in the Eocene with its early cats, dogs and elephants, the cool Oligocene on 29th December during which large mammals thrived. The Miocene saw in horses and Homo Australopithecus on 30th December in the morning, and the arid Pliocene with spreading Savannah and drying of the Mediterranean on the same day in the afternoon. The Pleistocene occupying the first half of 31st December was still dry and bore Homo Erectus and the Middle Paleolithic heralded in ourselves Homo Sapiens at 30 minutes to midnight. Some of us left Africa at 7.4 minutes to midnight and as the last Ice Age retreated we painted caves and hunted mammoths to extinction at 1.7 minutes to midnight. Jesus was born at 20 seconds to midnight, the Normans prevailed at Hastings at 9.3 seconds to years end and the Modern Age, 19th Century onwards endures from 1.5 seconds to years end at midnight 31st December. The complex recorded history of our species, so important to us, and the impressive technical achievements of the past three generations has occupied the final seconds of the year.

Life forms

What are we when reduced to our simplest constituents? Multicellular life forms exist in concept as a 'virtual lattice' determined by a 'blueprint' lodged in DNA. Onto the 'virtual lattice' the cells assemble and adhere in predetermined contiguity according to function, when worn replaced, ageing at a predetermined rate according to species until death and decay when the constituent elements leak back into the environment. The composition of the cells is in constant flux continuously exchanging elements, ions and molecules yet the chemical concentrations within the cells during life remain almost constant. The 'lattice' is 'virtual' as it is unseen even using the most sophisticated microscopes and exists only in concept not to be confused with connecting tissue which binds the tissues and organs and like all other tissues is cellular and formed in the process of embryogenesis, the development of the embryo from the fertilised ovum. The cellular relationships are maintained in the tissues and organs of the life forms whether plant or animal changing little with ageing until dissolution on death. In human terms people age but remain physically recognisable and retain an identity, develop unique individual mannerisms, consciousness, memories and relationships with other humans, life forms and the environment. The 'virtual lattice' and assembled cells are unique to each individual according to the genetic code with the exception of identical twins and clones as in the famed cloned sheep Dolly. The assembly of elements and molecules into even the simplest forms of life and the assembly of cells of differing functions into tissues and organs of plants and animals is largely unexplained by science and a modicum of humility remains appropriate whilst contemplating the mysteries of existence.

Out of Africa

Cave Paintings
Matobo, Zimbabwe

The San were archetypal hunter-gatherers capable of superb artistry,
a trait manifest within our species worldwide.

Out of Africa

The inspired insights of Charles Darwin irreversibly changed our world, shedding light on the origins of life and challenging religious orthodoxy. His Theory of Evolution can hardly be questioned in the light of fossil evidence and few deny that life forms have progressed from the simple to the complex including ourselves over billions of years. Darwin perceived that Natural Selection is the 'engine' of Evolution selecting those reproducing individuals of a species best equipped for survival in a hostile environment. Populations of a species differ widely in characteristics from the 'norm', be it in height or prominence of nose in the human species extending to ambition or indolence or in an insect species to resistance to pesticides. From natural variation are selected for survival those with most favourable attributes. Thus a species is refined to fit the requirements of an environment but profound changes in a species depend on sporadic changes in gene structure resulting from mutations in the germ cells of a reproducing life form. Such changes may be accelerated by radiation or other ill-defined environmental factors either favourable or unfavourable to the survival of the progeny which in turn determine the likely prevalence of the new gene in the species. The genetic makeup is known as the genotype which determines the apparent manifestation or phenotype. Most mutations are unfavourable, many are neutral or irrelevant and do not persist. Favourable mutations are much rarer. Major changes in a species require a <u>series</u> of complementary new genes and for such a constellation to assemble becomes statistically unlikely requiring many thousand or even millions of years to become a reality.

Mutations are more frequent in animals producing thousands of fertilised eggs during short lifespans with a rapid turnover of generations such as fruit flies and many insect, fish and amphibian species. Humans are generally capable of producing no more than ten children over a reproductive span of thirty-five years hence human evolution may be expected to be a very desultory process.

Africa, more specifically the Great Rift Valley, is regarded as the cradle of humankind from which Homo Erectus emerged 500,000 years ago and migrated across the still existing land bridge between Ethiopia and Southern Arabia to lightly populate the Near East and Europe. H.Erectus was much like ourselves, walked upright, utilised fire, made crude weapons, hunted and probably had the rudiments of speech but could not throw effectively, lacking the ability to rotate the forearm. He was well adapted to thrive as a hunter-gatherer in the African Savannah. Homo Sapiens evolved from the same African cradle 200,000 years ago in two subspecies. Neanderthalensis, a cruder, stockier, supposedly less innovative version than the newer current 'model' Sapiens Sapiens, ourselves, preceded us across the same land bridge into the Near East and Europe perhaps 90,000 years ago. Whether he found remnants of H.Erectus still surviving the Ice Age we do not know but 10,000 years later Sapiens Sapiens followed and annihilated or absorbed Neanderthalensis. H.Sapiens also spread from the Near East into Asia, and Oceana and only latterly into Australasia and the Americas. The qualities which set us apart from H.Erectus are far in excess of the demands of the African Savannah and could not have developed from favourable mutations over a mere 150,000 years between the supposed accession of H.Sapiens and the exit from Africa. The apparatus for speech of the quality we enjoy required huge anatomical adaptation in the larynx and coordination between the vocal cords, tongue, facial and respiratory muscles to create the nuances of tone, volume and timbre controlled by a highly developed speech centre in the brain and extensive neural connections. This complexity would require many 'good' mutations fortuitously arriving in time to complement the whole. The development would be impressive over a million years but virtually impossible to explain in Darwinian terms over a period of 150,000 years. No less remarkable are the uniquely human qualities which were already developed 80,000 years ago when H.Sapiens stepped out of Africa.

The evidence for this consists of attributes shared by all of humanity, by all races, from all continents which could not have evolved separately since the exodus from Africa a mere 80 thousand years ago. We share the same body language and facial expressions, a capacity for abstract thought, are able to share humour and engage in song, dance and the arts. We are able to learn the language of 'the other' and amongst all groups there are those with exceptional capacity to invent and excel in various fields... literature, architecture, medicine and engineering and extend the boundaries of knowledge into the realms of astrophysics and cyber communication. These abilities far exceed the skills necessary for humans to survive as hunter-gatherers in the African Savannah. How may we then explain the ascendancy of H. Sapiens? I cannot. Awaiting an explanation we should not be content with hasty 'fillers' nor gloss over the anomalies as if these do not exist.

Whence the spark which lit the flame?

Hunter-gathering remained the way of life for all of humanity over nigh on 100,000 years until the flame of civilisation flickered in the Middle East a mere 7000 years ago. It is false to presume that the early existence of cities, writing and architecture signal any ethnic superiority. China, India and the Mediterranean regions led the way while Western and Northern Europe were late starters. Australasia was separated from the spreading influence by ocean, Africa south of the Equator by tropical forest and further retarded by debilitating insect-born and parasitic diseases which hindered migration (read 'Bid the Sickness Cease' by Oliver Neill Ransford). The Incas and Aztecs of South America mastered impressive architecture and fashioned gold and silver artefacts but used stone to make tools and weapons. In modern times travel is much easier, migration readily undertaken and information easily propagated. The restraints to universal development are now war, ignorance and inequitable distribution of resources.

Finding fire

Making fire set the course for humankind not only to survive but to embark on the long road to civilisation. Fire enabled survival from the bitter winters of the Ice Age and cooking made nutrients in raw meat, grain, and vegetation more digestible and hence available for energy, overall health and brain development. Importantly less time was used in foraging and hunting and hence devoted more to contemplation and planning, social interaction and other activities. Notably human use of fire marked the first instance of tapping into stored solar energy by means other than eating plants or feeding on animals which eat plants.

Man is the measure

The Natural World has been moulded according to the needs, whims and fancy of our species. We love dogs, cats and horses for their practical use or because they are malleable and adaptable to our needs and to a degree reciprocate our affection. Dogs are pack animals as are we and lavish devotion on the human owner as a substitute pack leader who is comforted and flattered and often reciprocates with deep affection. We detest rats as these compete for our food in ways we find hard to counter, foul our living quarters and breed beyond our ability to control their numbers. We cultivate and adapt plants for food or for aesthetic appeal or practical use as medicines or for our comfort. We try to destroy and restrict the growth of plants which compete with our favourites and are indifferent to others which are neither of use nor compete. We dote on farm animals but kill these for food with little thought. We enjoy observing wild animals which we also kill for sport or cull if they threaten our food supply. Yes, 'Man is the yardstick'... inevitably, or we would not have survived as a species. However we are obliged to minimize suffering inflicted on the animals we exploit and restrain our power to destroy in order to preserve the web of life of which we are a part, or die within the web which would soon repair and start afresh without us.

Territory, War and Peace

"If I had a bell, I'd ring it in the morning, I'd ring it in the evening all over this land, I'd ring out a warning, a warning of danger, I'd ring out a message of love between my brothers and sisters all over this world ..."

(a campfire song of the 1950's).

Robert Ardrey, naturalist, dramatist and writer (Territorial Imperative 1960's) described territorial behaviour in many animal species manifesting in aggression across boundaries set by previous forays establishing an unstable equilibrium. Generally the resident group would prevail, confident in familiar territory, the trespassers ill at ease and quite easily scared off unless one group be weakened by loss of a leader or depleted in numbers or weakened by hunger or disease in which case the stronger would prevail. Fatalities or serious injury were uncommon, the defeated group would be incorporated or flee to seek 'fresh pastures'. Ardrey observed that a threatened group would become more cohesive, internal squabbling would cease and the leader accepted without challenge from which Ardrey deduced the dictum 'external enmity promotes internal amity in direct proportion'. Humans perhaps once behaved in a similar manner but success led to population pressure, territories became larger and conflict more bitter and cruel with massive fatalities in the defeated group, the survivors became slaves or concubines. Over the period of recorded history people were seldom during their lifetimes free from the fear of war. Robert Bigelow in his book 'The Dawn Warriors' describes the waves of conquest arising from 'hot centres' in which stable populations had thrived and proliferated over a generation, the best land was occupied, vocations were not yet diversified sufficiently to employ restless youth who rallied to the banners of ambitious leaders spoiling for the opportunities and excitement of war. The horsemen of Attila and Genghis Khan and the Vikings conveyed in their longboats swept through Europe in a frenzy of pillage and rape spreading their genes which are evident in the populations to this day. Settling in the depopulated areas the invaders thrived, raised families and often lived peacefully until galvanised by population pressure to again become a 'hot centre'. Bigelow makes another observation. Nations or tribes who were prepared to make alliances and combine forces were more likely to prevail. He goes further to presume that groups who compromise, exercise diplomacy and are capable of making alliances are more likely to survive and transmit the genes for self-control, logic and debate. He concludes that these genes are now more prevalent than ever before and that people should be much better able to settle differences and solve mutual problems amicably without resort to violence. In modern times Ardrey's Amity/Enmity equation can be applied to a common threat rather than 'an enemy at the gates' such as population pressure and depletion of and competition for resources. Modern warfare is so cataclysmically destructive as to blur any distinction between victory or defeat. There can be no winners. We already witness a progression toward international cooperation in the European Union which contrasts with turmoil and conflict over past centuries. India and China formerly consisting of cantons and city states are now consolidated into mega-nations maintaining a sometimes tenuous detente. North and South American states differ widely in ethnicity, language and forms of government, sometimes unstable but none are at war with one another at the time of writing.

*

African countries are mostly poor and many inefficiently managed but coexist peaceably apart from foci of turmoil initiated by Islamic radicals who also 'keep the pot boiling' in the Middle East.   Russia appeared to be moving in the right direction but is now regressing into medievalism, Iran is led by a clique of fundamentalists and Jihadists who have not yet emerged from a medieval mind set. Globalisation, ease of travel, migration, and rapid communication assisted by the ubiquity of mobile phones and the Internet have helped to dispel ethnic barriers and enlighten the world's peoples. The realisation has been grasped widely although not yet universally that more can be achieved through friendly dialogue and trade than by conquest. One may despair of ever achieving total international cooperation, awareness of the alternatives should sway the undecided. That awareness can only come about through education, informed and honest media and enlightened politicians and national leaders. When the majority of countries cooperate, seven eighths perhaps, the mavericks would be obliged to fall in line or risk sanctions and withdrawal of trade links and of aid. With consensus the major problems which confront humanity can be solved and the health of our planet restored however time is short and the matter is urgent. Despite evident cleverness mankind has so far failed to embrace the wider picture and master making peace rather than war.

The Price of War

War threatens the impressive gains in human achievement. There are no winners of modern wars. Maximal international cooperation utilizing the considerable available intellect is surely capable of helping to deal with the causes of war, the planetary problems of resource distribution or depletion, productivity, health, education and population pressure. Jihadism an immature medieval ideology and 'rogue' nations pursuing the agendas of power-greedy leaders retard and undermine the urgent resolution of these threats to civilisation. Time is short. The facts are inarguable but need to be clear and evident to all people and disseminated by whatever means. 'Start the ball rolling.'

Jihadism

Jihadism represents a relapse into medievalism, a regression into cultural immaturity, a stage in human development from which the civilised world has emerged.

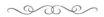

Conscience and Social Development

The babe's 'conscience page' is blank. The prevailing culture determines what is 'right' and what is 'wrong', starting with parents and extending to the family circle, family friends, teachers, associates and role models, imprinted into what Freud called the superego. Whilst the brain of the growing child is in what modern behavioural scientists call the 'plastic phase' receptivity and memory are maximal. Remarkable indeed is the ease with which young people assimilate the accumulated knowledge and culture to take their place as fully fledged members of a complex society, adept in navigating the intricacies of social interaction, vocation and technology.

Paradise

Alike for those who for Today prepare,
And those that after a Tomorrow stare,
A Muezzin from the Tower of Darkness cries,
"Fools! Your reward is neither Here nor There!"
Oh, come with old Khayyam, and leave the Wise
To talk; one thing is certain, that Life flies;
One thing is certain, and the Rest is Lies;
The Flower that once has blown forever dies.
Beyond the earth,
Beyond the farthest skies
I try to find Heaven and Hell.
Then I hear a solemn voice that says:
"Heaven and hell are inside"

Rubaiyat of Omar Khayyam (1100 CE) translated by E. Fitzgerald. (1868 CE)

Agonising over access to Heaven or suffering Hell in the afterlife occupied medieval minds. Modern minds are far less troubled over this issue and receptive to the reality that 'heaven' and 'hell' exist in the here and now and enjoyed or suffered by all sentient life accentuated in the human consciousness by long memory and vivid imagination. 'Heaven' embraces pleasure, well-being, contentment, love and sufficiency and 'hell' the obverse of the coin, pain, fear, illness, disability, deprivation, loneliness and despair. Troubled conscience and regrets send 'heaven' into retreat. We should be gentle with ourselves, repair what can be repaired, accept what cannot and strive for the wisdom to know the difference (ref. Serenity Prayer).

Avram's Discovery

4000 years ago in the Fertile Crescent between the Tigris and Euphrates Rivers in Ur, a flourishing Sumerian city, lived Avram, his wife Sarai, his aged father Terah and Lot, the son of Avram's deceased brother Haran. Three generations earlier the family had migrated from Haran (similarly named as Avram's deceased brother) a smaller city than Ur. Members of his family still lived in Haran having previously migrated there from distant Canaan due to drought threatening their livelihood as desert nomads (cuneiform tablets excavated in what was ancient Sumer recorded waves of Semitic desert nomads migrating to fertile Sumer). Avram and his family prospered in Ur and doubtless became more 'world-wise', probably acquiring land, a retinue of retainers and their families and were most likely to have been of Southern Semitic stock. Avram may have become restless and unhappy with the excesses and wanton behaviour of the inhabitants of the City and the lewd, cruel rituals including public copulation and human sacrifice enacted in the many temples dedicated to multiple gods. There were gods controlling most human activities, love, war, weather, harvests, the ocean, fertility and childbirth but none advocating kind, considerate behaviour between people and compassion extended to the stranger and the helpless. Perhaps in the quiet hours it occurred to Avram that the prevailing religions were of no benefit to humankind, the pantheon of gods varied from region to region and in truth did not exist, but rather a universal God, invisible, omniscient, without form or abode, benevolent demanding kindness and restraint between people according to guidelines which God would provide. Whether Avram interpreted the exciting ideas which entered his mind as spoken by God or whether God spoke in the literal sense depends on belief. Was he God's messenger and were Avram's growing family and accompanying adherents destined to be 'chosen' to carry the message however burdensome this task may prove? Did Avram himself believe or was the concept of one benevolent God demanding good human behaviour an intellectual construct designed to provide a moral compass for humanity? I rather think that he believed or he might not have been able to muster the energy and determination to pursue and disseminate a new religion. Did Avram and his family actually exist? The transition to monotheism was so abrupt in historic terms that it must have been the product of an individual mind at a time which coincides with the Biblical narrative. The name of the individual hardly matters but it could have been Avram! His genealogy as detailed in the Bible relates to very ordinary people not heroes or gods as in the mythology of most ancient cultures and the description of the sometimes dysfunctional family dynamics over four generations accords with the customs of the time and are entirely credible. Most families retain memories and relate anecdotes concerning deceased relatives over several generations. In the case of the Patriarchs the anecdotes would linger for generations related orally until written. Yes, I think it probable that the Patriarchs existed. From Biblical accounts we conclude that Avram was a born leader, possessed of vision, courage and charisma. He was also principled, kind and hospitable, however he was not without common human frailties exhibited less by Avram himself than by the women folk and Jacob, descendants of Avram's brothers Nahor who never left Haran the city and the deceased Haran who has been considered the possible husband of Sarai (who then contracted a Levirate marriage with Avram). The family genes were disseminated among the descendants of the Patriarchs and proved a potent combination which sustained them through future travails and the challenges in becoming 'chosen'. "Lech lecha" (Hebrew-"Go ye") God told Avram while he was still living in Ur and Avram 'went', sojourning in Haran with his family for an extended period before departing south with Sarai and Lot, son of Avram's deceased brother Haran, flocks he had acquired, beasts of burden and many servants, followers and their families, now a wealthy desert chieftain returning to his ancestral home in Canaan. He headed for Shechem (now Nablus on the West Bank of the Jordan). There God blessed Avram, promising that Sarai would bear a child and his many descendants would possess the land through which they were passing. The Covenant between God and Avram's descendants through the son Sarai would bear needed to be confirmed and sealed by a 'badge', circumcision of all male adherents of the new faith with which Avram complied, circumcising himself and all males in his household and in his service. Henceforth Avram ('High Father' in Hebrew) became Avraham (Most High Father) and Sarai would become Sara. Avraham and his followers were in a sense 'strangers' to the settled population (although 'coming home' after generations of absence) and were referred to as 'Ivrim' (Hebrews) meaning 'from beyond the River (Euphrates)'. The name stuck. Avraham sought a burial place for himself and his family and chose the Cave of Machpila near Hebron. The owner with whom Avraham was on friendly terms offered the site at no charge but without title however Avraham insisted on paying the asking price in full. The Cave and adjacent field became the first territory acquired in what was to become the Land of Israel. In time Avraham, Sarai and all the Patriarchs were buried there apart from Rachel who died near Bethlehem where her Tomb is situated and visited to this day.

Ethical monotheism in rudimentary form in Patriarchal times was refined through the agency of Moses and a series of Prophets, interpreted by Jesus of Nazareth and modified by

Mohamed and the Apostle Paul. Undoubtedly it is the basis of Law and Justice in the modern civilised world however it would be false to presume that there is no other basis for moral behaviour. Within any close-knit group whether family or tribe a code of behaviour to live by evolves to ensure harmony, enforced by the members of the group and inculcated into the young from infancy. 'The other' however is not consistently treated with the same respect and 'strangers' in a broader society or in a foreign land may be ill-treated with no pang of conscience. A belief in Karma associated with reincarnation effectively inspires moral behaviour and non-believers within a moral society absorb the ideals of that society. Do we still need religion in the modern world to provide a 'moral compass'? That is a matter for debate especially as religion has so often been exploited to justify the very behaviour which the religion seeks to abolish! Tolerance of innocent belief has to be a component of any moral code.

'The Binding of Isaac'... addendum

I have not included 'The Binding of Isaac' (Akedah...Hebrew) in this narrative as it is out of character for the Avram and the God we have come to know thus far, especially in view of the abhorrence over human sacrifice then prevalent in the known world. Scholars have detected a divergence in style and terminology relative to the rest of the Abrahamic narrative so it could be a later interpolation. To my mind the story has a dreamlike, nightmarish quality reflecting a conflict in Avram's mind between his love for his son and compliance to God's will. Could the story have originated in a dream which so gripped the listeners as to be repeated over generations and finally incorporated into the Biblical canon as an actual event? Dreams feature prominently in the story of the Patriarchs. Jacob's dreams are significant and recounted in detail… at Bethel on his way to stay with Laban in Haran and probably anxious and in a state of uncertainty he dreamed of a staircase rising to the heavens on which angels descend and ascend, when God reassures him of title to the Land to his many descendants, then again (he was a prolific dreamer) when he was preparing to reconcile with Esau. In fearful anticipation he dreamed of wrestling with an angel the whole night and woke at dawn with a painful hip and a recall that in the dream he had been renamed Israel (possible meaning…God Rules). And Joseph dreamed… and dreamed.

A Moral Compass

Whence will come a moral compass
For the many who have lost faith
In the Abrahamic God
Confucian wisdom and Buddhic belief?
Have we derived enough
From Biblical guidelines
To sustain us in perpetuity
A code of ethics, a moral sense
To restrain our baser innate impulses
Cruelty, lust and greed?
Who or what will protect
The weak, the widow
And the stranger
Feed and shelter those in need
Seek peace and not war?
From our vantage as we gaze
Into the past and our distant future
Can we muster the foresight and resolve
To pursue planetary cooperation
To stabilise our world, animals and trees
Oceans and soil
And maximize human happiness?
Now before it is too late
Consolidate what we have learned
During our staggered painful journey
Codify in manuscripts and microfilm
In Constitutions and in Colleges
Teach it in the schools, in places of meeting

In all languages all over the world.
Aim to sustain
The impoverished and the disabled
Uplift through education
Assist the ill, protect the weak
From harm and harassment.
The Law applying to all
Regardless of status or gender.
Infringement of Civil Law
Demands contrition and restitution
Infringement of Criminal Law
Brings punishment.
Punish the criminal
Not forgoing mercy
Nor kill nor maim to punish
Punish to deter and reform
Not as retribution.
Kindness and consideration
Although beyond the remit of Law
Are at the kernel of civilisation.
Ensure that all people
May exercise choice in electing their rulers
And contribute to debate
On the interpretation and exercise of the Law.
Only through an agreed world Constitution
Adaptable and dynamic
Continuously debated and reviewed
May we enjoy peace and plenty
Whether we accept or reject
The Abrahamic God.

Prayer

An earnest appeal, not necessarily in faith, belief nor expectation, a yearning, a plea, a desire or a wish, in defiance of reason and of natural laws, directed into the far reaches of the Universe from a point of consciousness into the endlessness of space constitutes prayer... from which finally to disengage with the unspoken thought "let it be". Is it unreasonable to appeal to a universal consciousness to intervene and alter the natural order of events, transcending our understanding of the physical laws of the universe? The appeal focused from the minute point of a single human mind into the infinite unknown is at once humble and audacious rendering the mind empty of extraneous influence and perhaps receptive to new realisation, hope and peace.

Empathy

Empathy, a capacity to recognise and to a degree share in the joy and pain of other sentient beings whether human or animal may be a purely human trait. Sympathy implies a capacity to share pain in order to comfort. Empathy is the basis for mercy and of equity which in law is applied to the tempering of punishment according to circumstance. Most people have capacity for empathy and sympathy and probably higher animals notably dogs, elephants and whales. A dog becomes subdued and stays close to a disconsolate human owner, elephants are solicitous towards ill or disabled members of the herd and evidently mourn their dead. Whales are more difficult to observe but appear to behave similarly. Although the majority of people have the capacity for empathy and sympathy, a few remain indifferent and a minority gain satisfaction from inflicting pain either as retribution to punish a perceived wrongdoing or insult, in warfare, or to satisfy an aberrant desire to inflict pain perhaps as a consequence of physical or emotional hurt in the formative years. Empathy understandably evaporates in combat. Is it empathy which prompts human kindness and moral behaviour? Is empathy an intrinsic part of the human psyche or acquired? These are rhetorical questions for which there is no clear answer.

A missed opportunity

What a missed opportunity had Paul the Apostle to offer the world compassionate, ethical monotheism unstifled by obsessive preoccupation with ritual, dogma and myth.

A First Rate Nation

A First Rate Nation is identified by certain criteria

◊ Rule of Law
◊ Independent Judiciary
◊ Multi-party Democracy
◊ Broadly Educated Electorate
◊ Freedoms of Speech and of the Press
  provided other freedoms are not impinged upon
◊ Freedom of Worship
◊ Freedom from Poverty (food, clothing and shelter assured)
◊ Freedom from Discrimination (over race, ethnicity, religion, disability, sex or age)
◊ Protection from Crime or Harassment
◊ Low Prevalence of Crime and Corruption
◊ Universal Education and Opportunity to realize full Potential of all citizens
◊ Access to Health Care
◊ Clean Environment
◊ Economic Viability
◊ Regard to Animal Welfare
◊ Militarily capable of Defence
◊ In the manner of a tithe a proportion of national wealth is set aside to assist the impoverished in other countries.

Britain fulfils these criteria and stands firmly amongst the Top Nations but there is always room for improvement!

Social Ills in early modern era UK

We have come a long way from Jack London's "People of the Abyss" (1903), an account of life in the slums in the East End of London of unremitting poverty, poorly rewarded toil, overcrowding, and inadequate food, clothing and shelter.

There is no 'free ride'

Ultimately work in human terms reflects the energy expended by people to gain the material benefits required to sustain and satisfy human existence. Hunter gathering by early humans or the research and intricate calculations needed to launch and direct a space probe are embraced by the same definition. Labour or the fruits thereof may be bartered or by recognised convention locked into coinage which is readily and conveniently stored and when opportune traded for a service or goods which sustain and satisfy human existence.

An enterprising person may save coinage and pay others to work for his/her profit. Circumstance which hinders workers in bargaining a fair wage is countered by checks and balances in the form of workers Unions and legislation. Capitalism wisely controlled utilises the initiative of individuals to create wealth permeating through society.

Civilised societies are taxed in order to provide services which sustain and satisfy the lives of the unfortunate who are unable to self-provide fully or partially whether through incapacity or temporary lack of opportunity. At all levels efficiency is ideally sought to obtain maximum benefit from work or from the coinage which represents work retrospectively. Waste is to be deplored and is rampant in our current 'throwaway' culture.

In modern developed society expectations and perceptions of entitlement run high extending to entertainment, food, the latest gadget or technology, exotic travel and early renewal of household goods. Poverty is defined by some as inability to afford these. Shorter working hours, early retirement, greater work satisfaction, support in old age and affordable housing are widely sought and democratically elected governments are under pressure to provide. Justifiable complaints are voiced on inadequacies of medical services, overstretched policing and imperfections in prisons reflecting shortages of staff and equipment due to shortfalls in the national treasury.

The 'cake' symbolising the wealth of a society is finite. Some individuals enjoy large 'slices' and some are so small as to barely sustain let alone satisfy. Government is in a position to even out the disparities through taxation and benefits taking care not to stifle initiative and incentive. Inevitably in a multiparty democracy the desires of the electorate may not be conducive for the greater good and it takes statesmanship and strong leadership to attain an optimal balance. In addition to wisely apportion the 'slices', a bigger 'cake' representing a vibrant growing economy must be the wider aim.

Ultimately, if excellence of medical services, policing and education, efficiently run prisons, security in old age and affordable housing are deemed by the people to be of sufficient importance then the required 'medicine', somewhat unpalatable, is a 'downscale' of expectation and perception of entitlement, abandonment of consumerism and willingness to work more efficiently for longer. There is no such thing as a 'free ride'. A word on defence spending… war is wastage of human endeavour and pathological in the sense that it neither sustains nor satisfies but renders null the toil of generations. Defence spending calculated to reduce the risk of war is therefore necessary and logical.

Economics, art or science?

As in the practice of Medicine, Economics is both art and science. An intuitive understanding of human behaviour is intrinsic to both, tempered by incisive reasoning, functions of both 'right brain' and 'left brain' (read chapter titled 'The Stuff of Dreams' in my book 'Reflections of a Sceptic'). Economists play a vital role in modern societies exemplified by the experiences of the past half century. Economies allowed 'to run free' resulted in two World Wars, the death of millions, cataclysmic destruction, poverty and a surfeit of human misery. The 'layman' might imagine that standard practice in implementing the necessary checks and balances would achieve economic stability yet the 21st Century has already witnessed a world recession and at least one economic 'meltdown'. Are these examples of 'economic negligence' with parallels in medical practice or expressions of the unpredictability of human behaviour? Clearly there is still much to be learned.

The Human Resource

Human potential, hidden, latent, ignored and undeveloped is a neglected, wasted resource which could be utilized to enhance the happiness of all mankind.

There are societies in which **women** are denied opportunities for education and participation in certain occupations and professions. Huge untapped potential lies latent amongst womankind.

Poverty denies opportunity to many young people due to lack of schools, qualified teachers and books and hunger or poor health of the pupils.

Discrimination in some countries in the past and currently denies education or entry into trades and professions to certain religious or ethnic groups.

Bureaucracy, inflated and superfluous sequestrates capable people from participation in the wider society in more productive roles.

Mismanaged systems of **education** may fail to guide youngsters in making appropriate career choices based on aptitude and the needs of the society.

The human resource is one of our most valuable assets, it is the foundation on which civilisation rests and is ignored at our peril.

Population control

We value the human resource but there is a 'tipping point' beyond which our planet cannot support more people. Population control is vital to halt the predictable trajectory into conflict over limited resources. Preserving the principle of sanctity of all existing human life is essential, for world peace is at stake. A descent into planetary warfare and decline in civilised standards is the bleak alternative.

The Limits of Reason...
as yet undetermined

Almost everyone is capable of rational thought, in fact rational thought directs most of our actions, whether we calculate what we can afford to buy or the shortest route to reach a destination. The scope of our reason is 'bite sized' limited to the problem in hand. Rarely do we zoom out to embrace the bigger picture yet the fate of humanity and the natural world depends on broad collective reasoning. The issues are not obscure nor difficult to understand but unless humankind collectively 'grasps the nettle' our complex civilisation will tumble like a house of cards in two or three generations. War, mutually destructive is threatened by resource scarcity or maldistribution, notably of food and energy, aggravated by uncontrolled population growth and the pursuit of selfish national or religious agendas. Pollution, destruction of natural habitat with the threat of global warming would all contribute to human misery. In the absence of *coordinated* effort a third 'Great Extinction' is threatened.

How may awareness of this real threat be communicated to the World's peoples, to the peasants who till the soil, factory workers, school children, writers and scientists, the educated and the illiterate and the politicians. An analogy is the kindling of a fire in a high wind using damp wood! Only with patience, persistence and some ingenuity will a small flame flicker fitfully and if nurtured eventually blaze and require feeding to be sustained. My efforts at kindling have been unsuccessful and I have almost run out of matches. Help!

At the Crossroads

We stand at the crossroads, pausing to read the signs to chart a course far into the millennium.

Seek a space in your busy lives to ponder, whether you toil for a pittance or enjoy prosperity, whether occupied with matters of family or pursue pleasure or novelty or survive under a totalitarian heel. Strive for a world in which peoples cooperate in peace and foreswear war, in which resources are more fairly distributed and positive action is taken in preserving the health of our planet. Although the nations may pledge to negotiate in peace vigilance remains necessary to deter any regression.

The Bath

I bask as in the tepid sea of an ancient planet

Easing away morning chill

In water energised

By combusting hydrocarbon

Bound by light and heat

Beamed from our star/sun

In aeons past

On vast ancient forests.

Miracle at Titusville

Upon the discovery of crude oil issuing from the earth
Near Titusville, Pennsylvania, USA in 1859
Is based the affluence of many.
Advanced technology and high ideals
Professed
But inadequately implemented.
A swarm of mosquitoes called to feast
Probosci pierce the skin
Of Planet Earth, sucking oil
The windfall recently discovered
Avidly fallen upon.
Whether an anonymous bequest
Or a random find
Thirstily sucking the straw
Until the final gurgle.
Slow down
There is a tomorrow.
Energy reliant
Our civilisation cannot be deprived.
Imperative
Is the pursuit of alternatives
Renewables.

Living batteries

Green plants
Living batteries
Store solar energy
In chemical compounds
Carbohydrates
Fossil hydrocarbons
Sustaining earthly life
Civilisation
Human survival
Warmth, cooking, hygiene
Materials, machinery
Manufacture and medicine
Travel, space exploration
Flowering of knowledge
Culture.
Chlorophyll the key

Green miracle
Photosynthesis.
In modern times
Technology
Enables humans
Using solar panels
To capture
Batteries to store
Solar energy
Increasingly
Bypassing plants
To save the forests
Cleanse the atmosphere
Reduce reliance
On fossil fuels.

Remarkable Chlorophyll

The molecular structure of chlorophyll, green bio-pigment, is characterised by a multi-angular 'ring' (consisting of 4 arrow shaped pyrrole 'lesser rings' tipped by a nitrogen(N) atom pointing towards a central metallic atom magnesium(Mg). Similar bio-pigments essential for certain advanced life forms are similarly structured but the central metallic atom differs... iron (Fe) in the case of haem as in haemoglobin, deep red in colour, essential for carrying oxygen from the lungs to the tissues in warm blooded animals. A central cobalt (Co) atom characterises the Vitamin B12 molecule, ruby red in colour, essential for the maturation of red blood cells. A central copper (Cu) atom in the ring centre occurs in the light green pigment haemocyanin essential for oxygen carriage in the blood of arthropods and molluscs (e.g. crabs, lobsters, snails). Myoglobin (red) which also has a central atom of iron (Fe), carries oxygen to skeletal muscle. The statistics relating to the development of diverse bio-pigments in such complex unique structure through the natural selection of random mutations stretches the capacity of the human mind!

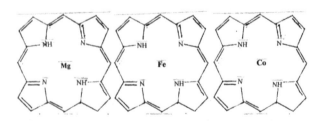

Le Chaim ... to Life

From the moment of inception of our Universe,
from the instant of the 'Big Bang' as we
conceive it, the process of dissolution began, the
dispersal of matter, the decay of its constituents
until ultimately there will be only energy,
endlessly diluted, dissipating into the infinite void.
The label *Entropy* is applied to this process of
inexorable decay. Life is a blip in this process, a
brief interruption, the integration of elements and
molecules into organic matter based on carbon.
Life is replicating, growing, mutating, expanding,
utilizing and storing energy emitted from our
decaying sun. Anabolism, the building up of
living material is the antithesis of decay, and
of catabolism in organic terms.
Entropy is, as we understand it, predictable and
inevitable. Life may be a brief 'blip', an isolated
incident in the vastness of space and time but
significant none-the-less, at least to an earthling,
as an interruption of the otherwise gloomy
inevitability of universal decay.
Appropriate is the Jewish toast
'le Chaim'... 'to Life'.

This we know – *the Earth does not belong to man – man belongs to the Earth. All things are connected like the blood which unites one family. Whatever befalls the Earth – befalls the sons of the Earth. Man did not weave the web of life – he is merely a strand in it. Whatever he does to the web, he does to himself.*

From the Declaration of Chief Seattle, Native American Chieftain 1854

Controlling Combustion, Saving the Forests

A billion years after the birth of our planet rudimentary life forms appeared in the oceans, neither plant nor animal, a million years later evolving into unicellular green organisms equipped with chlorophyll able to combine atmospheric carbon dioxide (CO_2) with water (H_2O), energised by sunlight into carbohydrate (CHO) e.g. sugars, starch plus O_2, both drawn upon to sustain the plants metabolism. The primitive plants became food for a separately evolved unicellular organism equipped with the means to ingest it and utilise the sugar and starch combined with O_2 to fuel its own metabolism, releasing CO_2 plus H_2O.

plant

$CO_2 + H_2O \rightarrow$ (chlorophyll is the catalyst, sunlight supplies the energy) $\rightarrow CHO + O_2$

animal

$CHO + O_2 \rightarrow CO_2 + H_2O$ (energy released to fuel animals metabolism)

The primitive plants and animals are the ancestors from which all later plants and animals evolved. Over many aeons an equilibrium was established between CO_2 and O_2 concentrations in the atmosphere, varying little over long periods. During the Carboniferous Era 350 million years ago vast forests resulted in rising oxygen (O_2) levels causing an `explosion` of animal life in the succeeding Cambrian Era extending into the Jurassic with its huge dinosaurs. O_2 levels fell establishing an equilibrium varying little over millennia until the advent of humankind.

Combustion played a minimal role over this extended period in altering the equilibrium, even the burning of wood by people for warmth and cooking made no noticeable difference until the discovery and exploitation of fossil fuels... coal, oil and natural gas... fuelling the Industrial Revolution in the 19th Century, we have no accurate records of CO_2 or O_2 levels at that time. Combustion intensified steadily during the 20th and early 21st Centuries until the present. Two World Wars, massive industrialisation, rising standards of living in many countries reliant on electricity generated by fossil fuels, millions of automobiles and the ubiquity of air travel have all contributed to continuing outpouring of CO_2 into the atmosphere. O_2 is consumed proportionately leading to slight but significant reduction of O_2 levels over large cities adding to the discomfort of sufferers from chronic lung disease however the public is less aware of this depletion than the unprecedented rise in CO_2 levels to which global warming, climate change and frequent natural disasters are attributed. In the current millennium the clearing of vast swathes of the world's forests by burning has had a dual effect, the combustion has contributed massively to rising CO_2 levels and as a result of fewer trees 'cleansing' of the atmosphere of excess CO_2 is impaired. The Amazon forests are said to supply 1/5th of the world's oxygen... are we risking a `die off` of the millions of city dwellers suffering from emphysema? Once destroyed regeneration of tropical forests would take more than a lifetime. At the time of writing, deliberate burning and clearing of tropical forests continues. World leaders are debating action but a sense of urgency appears to be lacking. Concerted efforts by Governments of leading nations are called for, such as offering monetary aid, assistance with policing, motor vehicles and surveillance aircraft or as a last resort trade sanctions or 'boots on the ground'. Surveillance by satellite and overflight by drones would help to monitor the status quo. The urgency of the situation cannot be overstated.

Ants, bees and us

Bee and ant colonies have been researched and understood for more than a century. Individual insects progress from birth into specific physically distinct roles as workers to gather food for the colony, as nurses to feed the young in larval stage, soldiers, male drones and potential queens. Roles are entered and performed instinctively without choice until death. Insect colonies have clearly evolved and naturally selected for survival relative to individual insects.

The planetary success of the human species is also dependent on group cooperation and even more complex diversity amongst individuals, physical distinction is less marked and largely independent of roles in society and freewill is exercised in the choice of occupation influenced by specific skills and attributes some of which manifest sporadically (or so it appears) but a genetic predisposition is often evident. Amongst higher mammals, wolf packs, meerkat communities and antelope herds have similar advantages in comparison to individual animals but the relationships within these groups are much less complex. Our species Homo Sapiens is unique in the diversity of talents, personal characteristics and abilities which have become increasingly evident with the growing complexity of human society as civilisation has evolved. This remarkable evolution is based on human diversity and a towering intellect far surpassing the endowment of our most recent ancestor Homo Erectus, a capable hunter-gatherer adapted to his Savannah environment. Human individuals have the free will to exercise their talents however in earlier times opportunities may not yet have existed, the shepherd with great musical potential could merely have created melody on a self-fashioned flute and the mathematician would usefully count his sheep and cut notches on a stick to record his tally… "Full many a flower is born to blush unseen ..." *Thomas Gray, 'Elegy Written in a Country Churchyard'* (1751). Greatly expanded populations yield correspondingly more talent and more geniuses. Ease and speed of communication, 'globalisation', the coalescence of populations into mega-states and the willingness to share knowledge have availed large swathes of the world's population the insights of Einstein and the fruits of prolific inventive genius.

Nicholas Christakis, writer and researcher in societal genetics postulated that human beings assemble themselves to form a "super-organism". Bee and ant colonies are recognised examples of superorganisms, amongst humans the concept appears exemplified by large cities such as Hong Kong which supports a population of over 7 million with a density of 57,250 per sq km. The city is confined by mountains and the South China Sea. The majority of the population live in high-rise buildings and on boats. Hong Kong is dedicated to trade but many people are employed in providing essential services, food and maintaining law and order despite gross disparities in income and living standards. The inhabitants display cheerfulness, and are bound by custom, shared ethics and family ties to live peaceably. The human superorganism contrasts with the superorganism of ants and bees being compartmentalized into national, ethnic and linguistic divisions locally governed but part of a greater cooperative dedicated to dialogue and solving difficulties and deficiencies amicably. Gradually isolated separate groups may be attracted to and join the coalition creating what might be termed an 'ultimate superorganism', disparate yet unified and unique, dedicated to a contented secure quality of life for all people and restoring our ailing planet to a state of health.

A dream without action remains merely a dream!

Hope

The 20th Century saw several bitter extended wars fought with sophisticated lethal weaponry which cost many millions of lives and mutual destruction of infrastructure. Memories of those conflicts linger and have encouraged a degree of peaceful co-existence and solving of differences through negotiation rather than war. The age of competition expressed in violence and warfare is on the wane as the age of progress through peaceful cooperation dawns. Through insight and understanding we can hasten that advent. There are hopeful signs on the horizon, in contrast to prevailing attitudes a mere three hundred years ago, most of the world nations pay at least 'lip service' to human rights and the dignity due to all people regardless of gender, race or religion. A mere 500 years ago the continents were populated by multiple small states ruled autocratically, with defined class divisions, the bulk of the population poor and oppressed, the states made shifting alliances and were often at war with one another. Gradually the states have coalesced to form mega-nations or federations, autocracy still operates but some form of democratic rule is established amongst more than half the nations of the world. Early in the 21st Century there are still opposing forces such as Jihadism and the hegemonic ambitions of dictators who strut and posture, threatening war oblivious to memories of death and destruction which attended conflicts in the region within living memory. We hope and trust these counter-productive relics of human adolescence will fade over succeeding generations and the human superorganism will achieve a sustainable equilibrium coexisting with other life on Earth and the planet itself, fulfilling the quest for *Tikkun Olam* ... Repairing the World. The pangs of transition accord with the long painful road already travelled, however time is short whilst the natural world is inexorably eroded and human population continues to grow. The existential crisis needs urgently to be brought to the attention of the Earth's people as a priority together with literacy, numeracy and whatever religious instruction is customarily given to the very young, regardless of culture or occupation. The issues should be clear, even to those without formal education. The energies of all people must be focussed towards a common goal, preserving the attainments of humanity and the health of our planet through discourse and cooperation foreswearing conflict. Peace revolves around limiting population growth, better conservation, distribution of resources and uplifting the status of the deprived as we would for our own families. Even totalitarian regimes are dependent on the will of the people, 'people power' cannot be overestimated. The movers and doers of society and religious authorities must lead the way. Perhaps readers of these essays may start the ball rolling?!